In the Human Zoo

THE AGHA SHAHID ALI PRIZE IN POETRY

In the Human Zoo

Jennifer Perrine

THE UNIVERSITY OF UTAH PRESS
Salt Lake City

Such Guts as Gifts

Howl

This Worm of Furnace

I've Never Swum with Dolphins

But once I plunged headlong into a pool
of jellyfish, ten million pulsing medusae
ushering me under the waterline,
where I buried my face in the sheer miracle,

not swimming but begging my legs to swivel
gingerly lest I tear their nimble blueberry
bodies, spill the light lurking in their eerie
mouths. Even blessed by the undulating opals,

caressed with tentacle benedictions, the fear—
not of these creatures, their tiny poison barbs—
but of my own graceless weight interrupting

their translucent, milky work, this severe
beauty I had the luck to wear, a living garb
that kissed my skin with its silk, with its sting.

A Transparent Man Is Hard to Find

After all, what teacher would want to expose
a horde of restive children to a glowing,
see-through penis, and so the science centers

of the world opted for female mannequins,
not simply nude but pellucid, her organs
wired to shine on command, even secretive

ovaries illuminated, twin suns sparked
by a well-timed switch. In the dark theatre
of adolescence, she emerged, virginal,

from billows of blood-red curtains, thunderous
voices narrating her internal workings.
I envied her—not the spotlit attraction,

but the body that behaved as it was asked:
arteries with their electric pulse, nerves strung
through her like blue icicles, incandescent

breasts made, the voices claimed, to be fed upon.
No amount of prayer saved me from my spindly,
stammering fate, and even worship would fail

to keep my icon ensconced: now she must rest
in the dungeon underneath this labyrinth
of interactive plasticized cadavers,

this oversized human heart I wander through,
its chambers so wide they echo each footfall,
each orison I say in its opaque name.

Portrait of My Mother as Mule

Am I that glistening drug you carried
across your borders, snug inside a condom

that burst the sheer sum of me into your blood?
When you swallowed hard and assented to smuggle

me into the world, did your secret tongue say
This will be the death of me? Or have I misheard

your name—did you believe yourself barren, burdened
by the weight my father foisted upon you, doomed

to carry his child like a pack that you'd been bred
to bear? And what then of the miracle birth,

the chromosomal misfit pilgrims traveled miles
to touch? What have I given you but a map

of your mixed roots? What have I taken but the grace
of knowing yourself as the last of your line?

Origin Story

Once, we were children in the forest. We were no Gretels.
We carried brooms to sweep our trails clean. No one could follow.

We gorged ourselves on bread, licked the crumbs from each other's lips.
We slaughtered songs to pass the time. The woods were populous

enough. We would walk until numbness spread from feet to shins,
to our lolling heads. We'd fall into beds of needles, leaves,

velvet moss. We'd wake again and wander, our tromping steps
freed from our overseer's odometer. We'd flown miles

from our begetters, fathers of brick, mothers of wicker.
Ever after, deep in the green slipped from the trees, we'd light

matches in the dark to keep watch, to warm our hands, to trace
in the spark and burn the outline of a familiar face.

Walking Home After the Graveyard Shift

Even the fireflies here are lochetic,
waiting to scoot their lemony asses

right up to my skin, to expose their short
streetlight sparks when I least expect it. Mace

and cloves from the bakery still dusting
my fingers, I grow talons of housekeys

that slash the August air, that sad frotteur
pushing against my shirt. Its little huffs

of damp wood and mud pour a fluvial
soup between my breasts. Behind me the owl

whistles its come-on, and I snap my legs
open and shut, a switchblade in the dark.

When, at Last, I Meet My Mother Again

her face clotheslines me, that jolt closing
my throat, so I never get to say

I remember her as a dragon—
whoosh of leathery wings and hot wind

by my ear, a scritch of crimson claws
against the tile—or am I this beast,

the way I've swallowed her whole, scraping
each bit of memory from my teeth?

Yes, I am this serpent, the glinting
scales, the snap and flex of jaw, this worm

of furnace I call tongue that wriggles
free to cut her again and again,

not the way St. Margaret hacked out
from the devil's belly, but the way

the reverent divvy up a relic,
splintering bone from bone, chipping limbs

into holy slivers they'll cling to
when the rest of the body has gone.

Wings Poised Like Knives

Portrait of Myself at Fourteen, as Saint Rose of Lima

Girl, I understood your temptations, your coveted face
rubbed down to red meat, the chili peppers scrubbing your cheeks

of each suitor's caress, shedding the glimmer of your skin,
your delicate hands, the ones you plunged wrist-deep into lime

then shoved in gloves full of nettles. How I envied your crown
of roses entwined with metal spikes, your hair-shirted world—

I had to make do with the tools of my time: the steak knife
I slid across my arms and ankles, anywhere their eyes

touched. When the first one came for me, I crawled into the cold
brick of my bed, waiting for a sign: I knew I'd been cleansed

when my blood dried up, when my hair cascaded from my head
in fistfuls of feathery wisps, when I could run my palms

over the flat of my chest and taste your words in my spit
like a bitter herb: *only pain keeps the Devil at bay.*

Senbazuru

Pain,
you've remade
me in your own image,
each day I'm reborn in your hands.
Where once my bones were silent and pink,
my body squared with its daily tasks, now I am creased
on your long, keen nail, you have doubled me over on myself.
You've filled me with folds,
mountains and valleys,
sharp beak jutting,   wings poised   like knives. Holy beast,
I am learning your art,
how your harsh geometries
bind into intricate designs: screaming crane, gasping fish, dragon
devouring its tail. If I let you name me one thousand times,
will you at last leave me exposed, let sun and
rain shred my thin paper to tatters
trained by the breeze,
let my wish be
released?

Palinode: Myoclonus

You sing my body
electric, pulse that tethers
me to the wakeful

world. Chalazae, small
knots at the ends of my rope:
how you hold my yolk

alert in this shell
where suns fall into my palms,
rise brutal as fists.

Thug, you muscle me
into your tics, your spastic
dance. Bouncer waiting

at the cordoned doors
to my hypnogogic trance:
three nights without rest

and my egg is cracked.
But benzodiazepine,
how sweetly it hums,

lullaby lacing
under my tongue, drowning out
your Pied Piper tune:

in sleep, I still hear
your shaky flute, the mountain
still waits to bury

me under its rock
and sway, your convulsive jazz
spilling from its cave.

Faint

The doctor says it's common to forget the minutes just before you fall. Still, you recall
the room igniting, bloody suns drawing rings in your vision, how your skin seared tight,
not even a fan to push air against your basted face, so your mind made
wind in its place, your knees refusing to fold, arms too weak to hold
your hands aloft, to cover your precious skull, ground growing
wild, fast, the floor now nearer, now so close you smell
the cedar, then the dull bliss, unaware
of that one moment lost, floating
in the dark sacred springs,
Our Lady of
Nothing.

This Animal Self

I waited as long as I could to wake you,
the cramps billowing out in waves so strong

I could hardly speak, let alone lift
my bones from the bed—so you carried me,

shuddering and doubled-up, down the hall
and knelt on the tile while I groaned and wept,

the burdensome skin of my clothes sloughed off
and tossed on the rim of the tub while I huffed

and strained and tried to imagine those microbes
mucking about in my gut, whipping

flagella like ribbon dancers, whispering
their secrets: *pili, fimbria,* all the ways

bacteria know to touch each other—
and when you touched me, pressing wet cloth

to my neck and kneading the cold dough
of my shoulders, I begged you to leave, wanting

to spare you the sight of my body
grudgingly toiling at its most menial

chore, to save you from the stench and the sound
of this dirty work, this animal self,

naked and hurt, and all the ways it might
return, how you'll be left to watch each disease

hatch in me, like an altricial bird
crying blindly, singing out to you.

When I'm Gone, Don't Remember Me

in this fossil of a body—
forget the dance of pills that worked,
then didn't, erase the bowl kept
by the bed to catch the water
I couldn't swallow, wring cold sweat
from the cloth you cupped to my flushed
skin. Burn all the films black, no trace
left of radiopaque lit up
in my brain, then blot out the stain
of your own knowing, how it spread
in you, too, its tendrils twining
into spindly nests where you hatched
your grief silently, fed its wide
and many mouths only after
I'd fallen asleep. Let those birds
die hungry along with me, keep
only two feathers, the barest
twigs, fragile fragment of a shell:
place them in a box marked *triptych*—
first, to name how we once had wings;
second, how even broken bits
last; third, a slick blue sheen of grace
to remind you: we both escaped.

Outside Paradise, Everything Is Other

Adam, this first day tossed
from the garden: even here

the song of dehiscence
comes scuttling up through fountains

of grass, all these anthers
bursting, clavigers loosing

their keys. Inside the weight
of freshly sinned flesh, pollen

spins its syrup, his breath
trickling from the honeycomb

of lung, fabiform nodes
in his neck germinative,

sprouting watery shoots
into blood, and oh, these bones

steeped in the lukewarm meat
of his skin say even this

is something to welcome:
even in this small wrestle

for each slow slug of air,
the body wants to be known.

The Beast by Its Harness

In the Human Zoo

I am no one's missing link, unless the gap
        they're seeking to fill is the synapse

between army-boot teen and batty old coot.
        Still I make a winsome captive,

even if I won't stoop to throwing my stool
        at passersby, won't perform

my traditional folk dance—cabbage patch,
        running man—for the gathering

crowd. Mine's not the quirky bodily wisdom
        of Chang and Eng, the fleshy wonder

of Venus, Hottentot or no, but I'm told
        when I smile I'm the spitting image

of Ota Benga, after clergy removed
        him from the zoo, capped his finely filed

teeth, dressed him in trousers and a bowler hat,
        christened him Otto, sent him to school.

Security Guard, Robert Gober's *Untitled* (1989–96)

People flock to see the haunted white gown,
      how it clothes no one yet rises, central,

voluminous, catches the light. Easy
      to keep busy, searching for beads and lace,

for the supports, the invisible stays
      that maintain this dream: purity at last,

no body to stand in its way. Few stop
      to gauge the weather in these walls: strange fruit

hanging against a periwinkle sky.
      These pastels soothe the eye, lull spectators

into the surrounding sleep—a thousand
      men safe in the house of night. I watch them

come and go, bite my lip, count to ten, drop
      my head to straighten the wayward tongue, gone

loose in my boot, to tug a brown sock high.
      The guests have declined a tour of my face,

never learn how I, too, can take up space
      but remain unseen while I wait, the clock

so slow each tick reminds me I should know
      this room will not let me leave, I'm wedded

to it, to this history, to this bride
      who promises there's nothing up her sleeve.

On Fallibility

When Pope Clement writes of resurrection,
            he compares it to the phoenix, a touch
of the virgin about her, a clean bird,
            no cloaca—hole for both excrement
and egg—but how lonely, *the only one*
            of its kind, perched like a stylite atop
her pillar of palm. Clement never speaks
            of how she spends her days, no brood to hatch,
no mate to seduce with her crimson plumes,
            no sweets to suck from flowers and fruit. No
abstemious girl, she devours pungent
            frankincense, plucks it up with her rose-gold
tongue—no mention of her fierce jaws carving
            the bark, how she waits while the resin bleeds
and hardens, how she lines her nest with scents
            fragrant and forbidding: cinnamon, myrrh,
spikenard. Clement sees her as miracle,
            but never notices this crime: firebird
at four hundred and ninety-nine, beak blunt,
            tail feathers faded to a patina,
crying in her sepulcher, her cradle,
            pause of the sun at dawn to hear her song.

Portrait of My Daughter as Pink Flamingo

Your tongue, too, will be a delicacy
in certain lands: this way of opening

to the world, upside-down, sifting single
cells from the silt and swallowing their names:

just saying *spirulina* can turn you
crimson, vermillion, all the rubescent

pleasures buried beneath your volcanic
lake, your water dance, your posture and bow,

your one-legged wink or firm-footed stamp,
how you joy to muck up the mud, to make

it hard to believe that some would love you
better as plastic bauble or mistake

your hard head for a tool to swing away
their ground bird sorrows, their unanswered songs.

Many Dangers, Toils, and Snares

On the sidewalk, crows strut in the sun,
starlets waiting to be discovered.

They surround me, this bench where I've stopped
for lunch, the bicycle I have spilled

at the edge of the field's zealous grass.
The crows have unfolded a possum's

skin, pluck its still red innards like seeds
from the pulp of a pomegranate.

Once, my mother told me God loves crows
more than all other birds—how they fend

for themselves, not just picking each corpse
clean, but erecting tools to torture

larvae from rotting logs, throwing snails
at the hard stones below to expose

soft bodies, whittling twigs to shiv grubs.
Here, in the summer heat, crows orbit

their noonday meat, satellites spinning
around a dead world. My cupped hands splash

water on my face, and I recall
how my mother would say grace: Hunger

is only the first of our trials,
God bless those who have learned to compete.

My Father's Parable

Over Thanksgiving dinner, my father remarks
        that my lover is built like my great-uncle Jack—
broad bones that look to burst the skin, hands thick

as Bibles—then proceeds to name Jack's misdeeds:
        drunken fits, worst of all the day he led
his donkey to till forty acres of field

and worked the creature until it fell, a heap
        of hairy dun. Jack unfurled a knotted rope
and with his full heft swung it, let it drop,

split that donkey's head like a melon left too long
        in the sun. My father shudders, remembering
the blood, how it shimmered in the soil, the tongue

lolling, how Jack hauled the beast by its harness
        all the way back to the house, pausing to curse
it for dying, to kick its ribs. When silence

falls on the table, my lover wonders aloud
        if my great-aunt watched her husband drag the dead
thing home, if she found a place to hide.

For Sport

Too long, I've been caught on your hook, underbelly wriggling
in the light: watch me flutter on your line, a kite exposed
to the wind's insistent beat, the sun's crease of heat slicing
sharp as a bone-handled knife. Your lips split, a generous
grin, when you refuse to reel me in, benevolent king
on your throne, lawn chair perched at the edge of a bridge, wild crown
of reflected asphalt haze bending arcs about your head.

I know I'm living on borrowed time: I count each dumb gasp
I heave until you unfasten me, throw me back. Mighty
god, pate turned purple as a turnip's top, jug of whiskey
by your side: in a daze, you've mistaken me for your bride,
liquid pearls lacing my naked throat. I can't outwit you,
but I can wait for your jittery wrist to shake me loose,
unthread your spool, my one reminder this hole slit clean through.

On Confession

I have pumped all my quarters into slots,
tossed enough pennies into sacred wells
        to know I have no luck. Chance takes his turn

    with whomever he pleases, and this time
he's led me to your hands, which shackle me

        to the wheel, launch clusters of cutlery
            toward my head: if you miss, it's a win,
but don't aim too high, too wide—spectators

        want the rush, the relief, slender closeness
of almost. When I leave, they want to see

        the target shot with woman-shaped holes, thrill
of a petty theft, as if they had picked
            the pocket of death, or stood astonished

    on the sidewalk while the trussed piano
slipped its rope and fell just shy, so they heard

        the clatter, watched the splinters fly, but walked
away safe. They've never asked how chance starts—
        white lilies in a vase, takeout in bed,

            bare bodies padding around unashamed—
        they only clamor for the tale's end: glass

    jar you broke against my head, my notebooks
            thrown into the fire, door I tried to bar
                behind me, the way I learned to play dead.

Just Enough to Draw Blood

Looking for the Tell

The first night we spent together, I watched
over your fitful sleep, not out of lust

for more of your dream-slack face, how your mouth
would open its heavy hatch to a realm

I barely knew, or how your eyes, flicking
beneath their sooty lids, would slip behind

a wayfaring thatch of blond hair. I kept
that vigil just to hear you snore—no drone

of sawed wood punctuated by murmurs
or beastly snorts—no, this was a colder,

an older sound that came up through your throat:
the clacking of dice in a fritillus,

thud of bills slapped down without heed of risk.
Yours was the row and racket of a breath

that didn't hedge its bets, that didn't mind
a gamble, that already knew you'd won.

Pentimenti

When we touch, it must be surreptitious
as when I snuck up to the Caravaggio

after the guard had left the room and plunged
my fingers down the dried streaks of the cardsharp's

hidden hand of clubs and hearts. I could trace
the pentimenti that flashed glimpses

of the cheater's former positions
the way I now brush the length of your inner

arm and feel the layers, a rush of marks
that crackle from the surface of your canvas.

How they make me want to strip you, scrape
my nails like a putty knife to unearth

each of your abandoned, half-sketched selves. Let
the accusers point, the alarms blare. I'll carve

through this thickness until you're bare, color
you with my own pigment, and will not repent.

I Found Love in the Hall of Mirrors

where you appeared like an actress in a film
  on a channel that I hadn't bought,
          glimpses of you distorted—now convex, now
        concave. I watched your curved dance, lurking
in corners and crowding me. You were so much,
  far and nearby: where I expected
         my own reflection, you were, unusual,
  confused, your many bodies rising,
            monumental—less Medusa's serpentine
              crown, carnival in its dizzying
      sway, and more obelisk, iceberg, fortified
    and cold, a regiment of soldiers
      stomping in lockstep. You looked hungry, licking
your lips, your tongue rough, wet as the gold
      meat of a plum. I tore out of your endless
     reaching arms, crashed through transparent panes,
not caring what ruins I made on my way
    to the mouth of the maze. Forgive me.
    I couldn't stay. I needed an idol, fixed,
   engraved, static icon on a wall,
        so I stumbled into bright sunlight, a world
where I worship in stark, silver planes
  an image of you cast back, flattened, a face
    I can possess in one level gaze.

This Page from My Pillow Book, This Page from My Bestiary

Mostly, I am elephant: thick-skinned, ponderous kiss
of flesh to dust. One ground my bones into a philter
for his own hard tusk. One taught me this pachyderm dance:
how to flaunt my sequined darlings, let them ride, limbs bare
as shafts of light. Mostly, they've said it's my choice: burlap
scratch of the poacher's bag, whirl of flash and cheers and whip.

Then, too, there's this: how I've been known to shapeshift, to stretch
these murky, membranous wings. One I lured to the mouth
of a cave to bathe in exodus: that flight that drenched
with its stream of screeching bodies. One I taught to writhe
at the sight of my face, its tangle of teeth. I track
them now with my voice: how it touches skin and bends back.

After He Breaks Her Arm

there's little I can do—the small conveyance
from the porch where she sat, one busted tooth
in her hand, to the hospital where she says,

car accident, just me, please, no cops.
In the harbor of my house, she sleeps
in my bed, the angles of her body wrapped

in my oversized pajamas, one sleeve
cut off for the cast. I wake her with tea,
burnt toast, runny eggs, though she winces

when she chews, the black whorl on her jaw
now haloed in green. Until her right eye
opens, I read her books, whatever's handy,

whatever keeps her here. Once, to cheer her,
I paint her nails, each a different color,
the enamel smearing up to her knuckles

when the crying starts again. The eighth night,
when she tells me she misses him, I'm kneeling
in the bethel of the bathroom, bent over

the tub, raking a razor through the thick
lather on her legs, and when she says,
take me home, I nick her ankle just enough

to draw blood, one rusty drop that slides
to the surface of the water, shimmies
its tendrils into the murk, and is gone.

Shivaree for the Bride-to-Be

There will be no honeymoon without my voice
thumping under your pillow the way
a shovelful of dirt batters a casket,

no first night without the clamor I'll summon,
each note heavy as a third body
in the bed. Let's say the gong of tire iron

on trashcan is just an amplified pebble
tossed at your window, a way to plumb
the depths of your nuptial sleep. Call it a gift,

this music, this swing band of wrench and kettle,
goodtime funk of fired shotgun, cowbell
wagging its insistent, blissful tongue. This night

spun with noise: sink into it like a needle
finds a familiar scratch, static skip
that drags us back, mouthing a morsel of song.

Apologia

Like rubbing hyssop into a bruise, there's always a way
        to make the blow smell sweet, the bitter mint radiating

into ragged wisps, the luminous names of broken blood—
        biliverdin, bilirubin—flooding your frangible

mouth, and when you return, she's marked with this too, her knuckles
        silky as bumps of wine, skin seared tight as if she might split

open like too ripe fruit—how you savor it even then,
        the soft give of flesh, the taste of something about to rot.

Such Guts as Gifts

Portrait of My Lover as Zombie

You come for me with arms outstretched, low moan
sloping from your hopeful mouth, hands that seek
the warmth of gut and blushing skin, wishbone
plucked from my bird-breast. On your tongue, the reek

of all the others you've devoured before,
their lips still kissing some secret chamber
of your slow-blooded remains. There's no war
in you, no want but that of the monster

to hunt until there's no more prey, to eat
without the need for hunger or the dread
of gluttony. I have no hopes to train

away this shambling seduction, this sweet
disease that whispers for you to embed
yourself in me like teeth inside a brain.

When the Dazzle Isn't Gradual

The Truth must dazzle gradually
Or every man be blind—

—EMILY DICKINSON

For every Greek god disguised as swan, bull,
eagle, ant, there's always a wolf dressed up
as divine, a seducer unwilling
to hold back, desire shining delicious,
mortal-vaporizing splendor from gold

eyes. We all know the kind, illusionists
who break open the everyday, replace
our skins with bright constellations, unleash
bears or scorpions or scaled dragons coiled
tightly where we expect ordinary,

unmarked skies. It's no trick of the light, smoke
and mirrors: where the lover touches us,
we are stunned, the self rent like threadbare cloth.
The lover summons from us an excess,
no mere pair of hares or doves extracted

from a hat, but a shower of silver
coins plucked from the air to the rhythm of wild
silence—no speech, no patter. We depart
new, grand, lost in worship, clapping madly
long after the houselights rise and curtains

drop, not knowing how we are the encore,
how this performance has left us transformed,
that soon we'll stumble upon some woman,
some man, unsuspecting, and manifest
as lightning, whirlwind, sight-scorching glory.

Maculate Conception

No more botanical metaphor—
spathe and *spadix*—no dimming the lights
on language. No summoning of gods
into the bedroom—*aeolian*
music of moans. Why not name the red
chafe of overworked lips, the errant
hair that slips back and forth in our spit,
slap and thump of stomachs like slackened
drums, fumble of shirts caught on our chins,
odd pops, squelches, underwear dangling
like lake trout from the line of one leg?
Why not celebrate the stain, wet spot
on the sheets, mark of how we were made?

Love Song for the Nutria

I've been told to be wary of you,
        how your carroty fangs will chew

through my truck tires and vinyl siding,
        even the cage where my neighbor tried

to force you to fight his frothing pit bull,
        riled for rodent flesh. I'm careful

in certain circles not to sympathize
        with your foraging, vespertine

ways, not to say how I love you best
        of all the bounty-hunted pests,

how I've watched your children, buoyant
        on the boat of your back, infants

plucking the nipples that ridge your spine,
        and imagined armies of you in lines

rising from the water like mammatus
        clouds in reverse, their pendulous,

icy breasts working a field of sky:
        coypu, go forth and multiply.

Portrait of My Daughter as Dominatrix

You demand and I obey, slipping a breast
out on the bus, the bony man across the aisle

grinning his all-gum grin. You make him wish
for a mouth as facile as yours, how you hurl

your salvo of howls until I bend to you, fill
you up. You wail on me, into me, those lungs

braiding air thick as a whip until I grovel,
crawl like a wounded pup to where you wait,

the silence when I suckle you heavy and red
as a palmprint on my cheek. You won't remember,

but I will, all those months you wore my skin
like so much leather, blood and cord tethering

us like a leash, and then the hours you tied
me to the bed until I came away your slave.

Fifteen Years Later, My Mother Apologizes

for leaving me like a bloody thumbprint on the wall. *Better*
       late than never, she says, though what's *better* but a bit of grit

to pumice the rough husk of my palm, what's *never* but a book
       turned to dust on the shelf, the rusty knell of her voice rasping

from cell to cell, whittling a space like a wound through the air
       to where I sit, listening to the surreptitious whistle

of time, how it flies: not as an arrow cleaving its sharp heart
       into a buck's back, not so certain as that. Time flew for us

with tremulous, sputtering wings, with a sound like crows spilling
       up from the corn, with the urgent lurch of a gut or a fist

or a kiss rushing up in the warm, round night. Time swirled my tongue
       like ribbon in its talons, left these satin shreds I circle

around my mother now, spinning them tight against the maypole
       of her regret, plaiting their threads into some garland of harm,

some murderous word I'll unearth, evidence that I am hers.

Portrait of Myself as Precious Stone, as Accident
Waiting to Happen

When I sense you looming on the other end—
a jeweler fisheyed through a loupe—I glitter,
each facet winking under its lash of light.

When I say *marvel, revel in these bevels,*
I mean *oh, how you've cut.* I mean I've never
been so much ornament as marcescent frond

clinging to the green, never so much emerald
as that lovat bit of bottle glass buried
in your heel. Leave me here, or don't—either way

you're shot through with luster, this glint I've murmured
into your blood. Let the wound wear its brilliant
flash of scar as boast, as a terrible crown.

Maggot Therapy

If only I could introduce you to all my wounds
       to work your healing art, to debride this necrotic

part every medic has tried to restore. Let me add
       you to my armamentarium, to all the ways

I've excised this grief, to the panoply of magnets
       and massage, twelve steps and hypnosis, sex, drugs, and rocks

of rough words sunk to plumb this well. You could colonize
       each burn left by a lover's tongue, fingers frostbitten

by their own frigid touch, the bone marrow infection
       of regret. I'd let you feast until we both transmute:

you into green bottle fly, scintillant buzz and speck
       of miracle, and I'll come through, too, as gleaming pink

tissue, as living flesh marked by your digestive kiss,
       remnant of the damage where you wriggled with delight.

Nothing Gets Me Hotter than a Punch in the Face

That's just how she says it—the way I'd say
I could survive on fresh mangoes alone,

or *I should quit school and start a commune*—
always that wistfulness, eyes sunspotted

with impossibility, the level
gaze of Lot's wife into the horizon

just before she spun round and begged the fire
to swallow her too—but there's no turning

back from this revelation, this gauntlet
she's cast into our seventh date, after

homemade ice cream and three hours of sitcoms,
after nuzzling sweet and soft as a peach,

after her looming face, its alien
topography in orbit around me,

and the dust storm of her body silting
my mouth: this is the last moment before

I learn my hands can break like bricks of clay,
before I become bits of asphalt lodged

in her tender skin, before she marks me,
her tendril of chalk skating down my slate.

Intersections

We were just two women in a car, and at each stop sign,
you'd preen in the rearview mirror, conducting your orange
anime hair, touching up your violent rouge. Everything
about me was tight and brown: I obeyed the stringent laws
of soap and salon. Between intersections, you began
to fold my love poem into an airplane, its terraced
wings crisp, as you steered with your knees. This, our common era,
when I accepted such guts as gifts, when I would let you
reach for me and pull out what you needed. At the last turn
before you took me home, you flicked your light flying machine
out the window, said, *let's see how far this baby will go.*

Cicatrix

You teach me a new word for *scar*, scissor
      it into my mouth, where I whisk it about, test

the crunch of it between my teeth the way
      in sixth grade my friend Noreen buried her canines

deep in my left wrist, leaving two pale bumps
      that rise from my skin, pink inchworms humping from bone

to bone. I'd done her wrong, perching a kiss
      on her beloved's cheek, and I'm no better now,

hiking up my skirt to reveal the knee,
      the thigh, the visible stripe where the upthrust head

of a nail married my flesh. You don't touch,
      but etch the name into the thick bark of my brain,

leaving a mark to surface when I search
      for that way to say *healed* that holds fast to the wound.

Howl

Portrait of My Mother as Kitchen Utensil

It's as if I'm living in a stranger's house
        where I can trawl the kitchen for hours

for something so mundane as a mixing bowl
        or spatula, inserting my whole

body into a cupboard to dig behind
        a blender, groping through a drawer to find

only carving knives and two-tined forks. I hunt
        for you like this: as if I'm the one

who's been misplaced, forced into a strange landscape
        where I expect to unearth your shape

in all its usual haunts. If I don't spot
        you in your chair, your bed, running hot

water into the sink, I'll look in a less
        likely place: in the folds of a dress

where I bury my face, in this breath that aches
        towards sleep, in the clock that takes and takes.

Majie

—*Chinese, "to curse the street"*

The third night you didn't come home, I hauled
boxes of dishes up from the basement—
your mother's wedding crystal, the yellowed

stoneware from Goodwill—every piece once held
to someone else's lips, rubbed by foreign
fingers. From the balcony, I began:

first, the snifters, still brimming with the scent
of brandies I'd never had, the slight whirr
and ting of their tapered mouths opening

against the pavement. Then the saucers, flutes,
cereal bowls: their slivers strewn like seed
for some industrial bird. In neighbors'

houses, blinds flew up, light streaking the arcs
of whirling discs, empty cups, the hard flight
of a curse into the air. I can't say

what names I made that night for the street's bold
betrayal, how it sprawled before our door,
its stone skin waiting to take you away.

Portrait of My Lover as Medium

You say the best way to know me is to summon
       all my ghosts, and so your throat learns the voice
of the boy I kissed behind the shed, who ten

years later sailed his kid brother through a windscreen,
       then shot himself. It's uncanny how you sound out
the notes, the way he'd say my name, even your spit

conjuring up the tinny taste of his braces.
       Sometimes, instead, you let my grandmother's muscles
live under your skin: how you move with the grace

of forty years' work, your hands harvesting, shucking
       clothes, shelling me, your sweat scented with soil,
scrubbed in sun. And then the dead you know best of all:

the daughter who won't come when called, your face worn
       with the task of tuning into that lost channel,
a silent static spooling behind your eyes.

Refuge

We take shelter from the soaking night, duck down
  an alley, find an awning. *Why must we skulk*

       about like this? I expect you're scared, want more
          privacy—instead you say, *Skulk is a group*

    of foxes. I think it's *troop*, but don't argue,
reach to run my hands through your bristled crew cut:

   How did you feel when they shaved it? You laugh, *dis-*
tressed, then start—a raccoon has crashed the trashcan

     behind you, carrion clutched tight in its jaws.
      In the dark, your lighter clicks, exhales, draws out

  the sweet stink of smoke. Before you snuff the brief
flame, your scar is visible, a grey runnel

    through the downy hair on your arm. I hold you
   in silence, while around us the full city

 roars, steam chuffing from grates, whole generations
    of rats scuttling behind the bricks of the wall

      on which we lean, rain falling like an angry
      baptism to protect us from whatever gods

  have followed us from our pasts to this new place.

If Life Gives You Lemons, Make

your mouth into a trough, a spout
from which that sour sauce will pour,
pulp and spittle swimming down your
chin, eyes pinched shut, each acid thought

welling under the tongue. Thin slice
of pain wedged on the salty rim
of your face, let its tart grace skim
your glass neat: no sugar, no ice

to temper this bite, this slick burst
that cankers your lips. Life gives you
lemons: cut your teeth on their rinds,

tear them with gusto, slake your thirst
with their slavering, jaundiced juice,
swallow hard, leave no seeds behind.

Apology for My Recklessness

I kept the vase you gave me
        just before I left,
the one you shaped and sintered
        into almost black
glass—now, the sunlight that spills
        into my new home
imparts the hard glaze a gloss
        like skin pulled taut. Guests
marvel at its lute body,
        the lines you incised
with care not to cut clean through—
        only I can know
the side I've turned to the wall,
        the fluted mouth cracked
when I so hastily packed,
        fragile part I try
to hide so others can see
        what you made for me
as you wanted it: complete.

Mother, Self-Portrait, 2006

In the last photograph of my mother,
the borders are blurred into a vignette,

and though it's a twenty-first-century
print, she's tinted herself with sepia.

Still, her leopard-spot outfit gasps, golden
sheen of glitter bright in the fading light,

drawing my eye from her half-fallen face,
the places the aneurysm kissed so hard

her muscles buckled. From this safe distance,
I can trace the undone bow of her mouth,

left side of her lips a loose string dangling,
toy on a slack tether. Though they were made

only through the phone, I can see now how
her apologies were formed, the struggle

to shape the words at all, drop of spittle
weeping down her chin, how she would knuckle

its thin thread as she spoke. In this picture,
the last one she sent, her gaze won't let me

resent any longer the missing years,
the ones that brought her into this soft skin,

this hair gone white, the ones that carried her
to this stoop on a house I've never known,

steps where she's perched like a pigeon, tiny
and grey, ready to wing its long way home.

Aubade

Dawn came coral as a reef running
    like a rib under the skin of the sky, sliced
        the black open, wicked wound, blood blown
    across the surface of the day. She flirted
through curtains, made her way through our room
    as a calm breeze sweeps cleanly across the town
        just after the tornado's touched down.
    We uttered oaths, made lewd gestures—still she beat
her bird body against our windows—
    so we tried disguises: cons with slick come-ons
        swindling one last dollar from the dark,
    devils endeavoring to outscorch the sun,
but our horns were dulled by caresses,
    eroded by the rub of silk. Let's face it:
        we're no tricksters, no bold warriors,
    though we fought, our teeth bared, claws tearing the light.
We're no fools either: if we can't hold
    back morning, we'll lean into it, invent new
        languages where every word means night.

Dear Lindy and Balboa, Dear Charleston and Shag,

In the year when intimacy
       was a stranger, when all my flesh
              was stiff as an unused mattress,
                     you taught me abandon through swing,

jazz shimmering syncopated
       heat, crotchets and quavers delayed,
              relaxed, both languorous and fast.
                     In close embrace, or side by side,

you would glide, improvise, circle
       yourself around my quaking frame,
              my arms and hips all nervous shake,
                     my brow furrowed, an amateur

carpenter leveling each beam,
       taking care each joist is square. Hooked,
              you raised me aloft, into song,
                     where I was almost bodiless,

an arch in the air, graceful sweep,
       my huddled, hunkered limbs unfurled
              as if I could climb the wind, gain
                     entrance to some ethereal

dance floor that shudders, energy
       emanating from this voltage
              of feet unleashed like a pent howl
                     by your unpredictable beat.

Acknowledgments

I offer grateful acknowledgment to the editors who have supported my work over the years. In particular, I would like to thank the staff of the journals in which these poems first appeared, some in earlier forms:

Atlanta Review: "Maculate Conception," "Portrait of My Daughter as Dominatrix"

Bellingham Review: "Many Dangers, Toils, and Snares," "When the Dazzle Isn't Gradual"

Black Warrior Review: "Portrait of My Daughter as Pink Flamingo"

Connecticut Review: "I've Never Swum with Dolphins," "Portrait of My Lover as Zombie"

Crab Orchard Review: "Portrait of Myself at Fourteen, as Saint Rose of Lima"

Cream City Review: "Portrait of My Mother as Kitchen Utensil," "Walking Home After the Graveyard Shift"

Ellipsis: "Nothing Gets Me Hotter than a Punch in the Face"

Georgetown Review: "My Father's Parable," "Origin Story"

Green Mountains Review: "After He Breaks Her Arm," "Apologia," "When, at Last, I Meet My Mother Again"

Harpur Palate: "Aubade"

The Journal: "Outside Paradise, Everything Is Other"

The Ledge: "Love Song for the Nutria," "Portrait of My Lover as Medium," "Portrait of Myself as Precious Stone, as Accident Waiting to Happen," "A Transparent Man Is Hard to Find"

Paterson Literary Review: "Intersections"
River Styx: "Shivaree for the Bride-to-Be"
Smartish Pace: "When I'm Gone, Don't Remember Me"
Spoon River Poetry Review: "Fifteen Years Later, My Mother Apologizes"
Sycamore Review: "Majie"
Third Coast: "Portrait of My Mother as Mule," "This Animal Self"
Unsplendid: "This Page from My Pillow Book, This Page from My Bestiary"

"Cicatrix," "In the Human Zoo," and "Maggot Therapy" first appeared in the Poetry Center of Chicago's Fourteenth Annual Juried Reading chapbook, published by Dancing Girl Press. "If Life Gives You Lemons, Make" first appeared on the Poetry Daily Web site and as a limited edition, letterpress broadside created by the Virginia Arts of the Book Center. "Many Dangers, Toils, and Snares" also appeared as a limited edition broadside published by the Center for Book Arts. "Mother, Self-Portrait, 2006" first appeared on the Web site of the Dorothy Sargent Rosenberg Poetry Prizes.

I owe sincere thanks to my mentors and colleagues for their support of my writing over the years. In addition, this book would not exist without my students, who remind me daily how to be vulnerable, how to be wild. I am especially grateful to residencies from the Kimmel Harding Nelson Center for the Arts, during which this book first began to take shape, and the Midwest Writing Center's Great River Writer's Retreat, which afforded me the space and time to discover new paths for these poems. Thanks also to the Center for the Humanities at Drake University for providing me with a course release to complete and revise this book. Much gratitude to everyone at the University of Utah Press, especially Jessica Booth for the beautiful book design, and Peter DeLafosse for overseeing the whole process. Particular thanks to Kate Coles of the University of Utah's Department of English for her insightful final edits. I am indebted to Anne Winters for selecting the book for publication and for her kind words. Susanna Childress and Sara Pennington have my endless appreciation for their friendship, wisdom, and encouragement—you keep me buoyant both personally and poetically. Howls to Frank, Von, Blake, Bean, and TJ, for keeping me in touch with my animal self. And always, love to Justin Huck, for dazzling me.